Let's Get Cooking

STUDENT
COOKBOOK

Over **100** easy-to-follow recipes

GW00336620

igloobooks

igl/oobooks

Published in 2017
by Igloo Books Ltd
Cottage Farm
Sywell
NN6 0BJ
www.igloobooks.com

Designed by Nicholas Gage
Edited by Jasmin Peppiatt

All imagery © iStock / Getty Images

REX001 0617
2 4 6 8 10 9 7 5 3 1
ISBN 978-1-78670-865-6

Printed and manufactured in China

Contents

Breakfasts

Strawberry Yogurt Breakfast Pots

75 g / 2 ½ oz / ½ cup strawberries
1 tsp runny honey
2 tbsp Greek yogurt
½ tsp demerara sugar

1. Slice the strawberries and put them in a small kilner jar.
2. Stir the honey into the yogurt and spoon on top, then sprinkle with sugar.
3. Seal the kilner jar and store in the fridge overnight, ready to be enjoyed as a speedy breakfast the next day.

SERVES: **4** | PREP TIME: **10 MINS** | COOKING TIME: **8 MINS**

Banana and Maple Syrup Porridge

2 large ripe bananas
600 ml / 1 pint / 2 ½ cups whole milk
125 g / 4 ½ oz / 1 ¼ cups rolled
    porridge oats
2 tbsp maple syrup, plus extra for drizzling

1. Mash one of the bananas and mix with the milk and oats in a saucepan. Stir over a medium heat until it starts to simmer.
2. Add the maple syrup and a pinch of salt then reduce the heat to its lowest setting and continue to stir for 5 minutes.
3. Divide the porridge between four bowls.
4. Slice the other banana and divide between the bowls, then drizzle with extra maple syrup to taste.

SERVES: **2** | PREP TIME: **5 MINS** | COOKING TIME: **5 MINS**

Scrambled Egg on Toast

2 slices granary bread
2 tbsp butter, softened
4 large eggs

1. Toast the bread in a toaster or under a hot grill until golden brown. Spread with half the butter and keep warm.
2. Gently beat the eggs with a pinch of salt and pepper to break up the yolks.
3. Heat the rest of the butter in a non-stick frying pan until sizzling then pour in the eggs.
4. Cook over a low heat, stirring constantly until the eggs start to scramble. As soon as it reaches your favourite scramble consistency, divide it between the two slices of toast and serve immediately.

SERVES: **2** | PREP TIME: **5 MINS** | COOKING TIME: **10 MINS**

Poached Egg and Pea Toasts

50 g / 1 ¾ oz / ⅓ cup frozen peas or a mixture of peas, broad beans and edamame
2 tbsp white wine vinegar
2 large very fresh eggs
2 slices crusty bread
50 g / 1 ¾ oz / ¼ cup soft goat's cheese
1 handful pea shoots
25 g piece Pecorino or Parmesan

1. Bring a wide saucepan of water to the boil and cook the peas and beans for 4 minutes. Transfer to a bowl with a slotted spoon.
2. Reduce the heat of the pan to a gentle simmer and stir in the vinegar.
3. Crack each egg into a cup then pour them smoothly into the water, one at a time. Poach gently for 3 minutes.
4. Toast the bread until golden, then spread with the goat's cheese. Mix the peas and beans with the pea shoots and spoon them on top.
5. Remove the eggs from the pan with a slotted spoon and blot dry with kitchen roll before laying them on the toast.
6. Use a vegetable peeler to shave over the cheese and serve immediately.

SERVES: **4** | PREP TIME: **10 MINS** | CHILLING TIME: **8 HOURS**

Overnight Muesli with Berries

125 g / 4 ½ oz / 1 ¼ cups rolled porridge oats

50 g / 1 ¾ oz / ¼ cup whole oat groats

50 g / 1 ¾ oz / ¼ cup sunflower seeds

50 g / 1 ¾ oz / ¼ cup flax seeds

50 g / 1 ¾ oz / ¼ cup hulled hemp seeds

2 tbsp runny honey

500 ml / 17 ½ fl. oz / 2 cups whole milk, plus extra to serve

200 g / 7 oz / 1 ⅓ cups mixed berries, sliced if large

100 ml / 3 ½ oz / ½ cup natural yogurt

1. Mix the oats with the groats and seeds and set aside 2 tablespoons of the dry mix.
2. Stir the honey into the milk to dissolve, then stir it into the oat mix. Leave to soak overnight in the fridge.
3. Stir the muesli well and divide between four bowls, adding a little extra milk to loosen if needed.
4. Top each bowl with berries and a spoonful of yogurt, then sprinkle with the reserved oat mix.

SERVES: 4 | PREP TIME: 15 MINS | COOKING TIME: 30 MINS

Banana and Walnut Pancakes

250 g / 9 oz / 1 ⅔ cups plain
(all purpose) flour
2 tsp baking powder
4 very ripe bananas
2 large eggs
225 ml / 8 fl. oz / ¾ cups milk
2 tbsp melted butter
125 ml / 4 ½ fl. oz / ½ cup golden syrup
50 g / 1 ¾ oz / ½ cup walnuts, chopped

1. Mix the flour and baking powder in a bowl and make a well in the centre.
2. Mash two of the bananas with a fork until smooth, then whisk in the eggs and milk. Gradually whisk the mixture into the flour bowl. Melt the butter in a frying pan then whisk it into the batter. Put the buttered frying pan back over a low heat.
3. Spoon heaped tablespoons of the batter into the pan and cook for 2 minutes or until small bubbles start to appear on the surface. Turn the pancakes over with a spatula and cook the other side until golden brown and cooked through.
4. Repeat until all the batter has been used, keeping the finished batches warm in a low oven.
5. Stack the pancakes on warm plates. Slice the other two bananas and arrange on top with the walnuts, then drizzle with golden syrup.

Fresh Fruit Muesli Jars

125 g / 4 ½ oz / 1 ¼ cups rolled
    porridge oats
50 g / 1 ¾ oz / ¼ cup whole oat groats
50 g / 1 ¾ oz / ¼ cup flax seeds
50 g / 1 ¾ oz / ¼ cup hulled hemp seeds
50 g / 1 ¾ oz / ¼ cup sunflower seeds
2 tbsp runny honey
500 ml / 17 ½ fl. oz / 2 cups natural yogurt
200 g / 7 oz / 1 ⅓ cups mixed berries,
    sliced if large

1. Toss together the oats, groats, flax, hemp and sunflower seeds in a mixing bowl.
2. Stir the honey into the yogurt, then layer up inside four jars with the oat mix and berries.

Smoked Salmon Bagels

2 seeded bagels, halved horizontally
2 tbsp cream cheese
4 slices smoked salmon
1 lemon wedge
2 lettuce leaves

1. Spread the bagel bases with cream cheese and arrange the smoked salmon on top.
2. Squeeze a little lemon juice over each one and top with lettuce.
3. Put the bagel tops on top and serve immediately.

SERVES: **2** | PREP TIME: **5 MINS** | COOKING TIME: **2 MINS**

Banana, Cranberry and Walnut Toasties

2 tbsp butter, softened
1 tsp icing (confectioner's) sugar
½ tsp ground cinnamon
2 tbsp walnuts, finely chopped, plus extra to garnish
4 slices white bloomer
2 bananas, halved
50 g / 1 ¾ oz / ¼ cup dried cranberries, plus extra to garnish
mint leaves, to garnish

1. Preheat a toasted sandwich maker or put two cast iron frying pans over a medium heat.
2. Mix the butter with the icing sugar, cinnamon and walnuts and spread it over the bread.
3. Sandwich the bread together with banana and cranberries.
4. Toast the sandwiches in the sandwich maker or put them in one of the frying pans and sit the other on top. Toast for 2 minutes or until the bread is golden brown.
5. Cut the toasties in half and serve garnished with walnuts, cranberries and mint.

SERVES: 4 | PREP TIME: 5 MINS | COOKING TIME: 25 MINS

Berry and Cashew Pancakes

250 g / 9 oz / 1 ⅔ cups plain (all purpose) flour

2 tsp baking powder

2 large eggs

1 orange, zest finely grated

300 ml / 10 ½ fl. oz / 1 ¼ cups milk

2 tbsp butter

150 g / 5 ½ oz / 1 cup mixed berries

50 g / 1 ¾ oz / ½ cup roasted cashew nuts

icing (confectioner's) sugar for dusting

pouring cream, to serve

1. Mix the flour and baking powder in a bowl and make a well in the centre. Break in the eggs, add the orange zest and pour in the milk, then use a whisk to gradually incorporate all of the flour from round the outside.

2. Melt the butter in a small frying pan then whisk it into the batter.

3. Put the buttered frying pan back over a low heat. Spoon the batter into the pan and cook for 2 minutes or until small bubbles start to appear on the surface.

4. Turn the pancakes over with a spatula and cook the other side until golden brown and cooked through.

5. Repeat until all the batter has been used, then stack the pancakes onto plates and garnish with berries and cashews. Sprinkle with icing sugar and serve with a jug of pouring cream on the side.

Toasted Ham and Cheese Muffin

2 slices processed cheese
1 English breakfast muffin,
  halved horizontally
3 slices cucumber
3 small slices smoked ham

1. Preheat a panini press or toasted sandwich maker.
2. Lay a slice of cheese on the bottom half of the muffin and top with cucumber.
3. Fold the ham slices in half and arrange on top, then add the other slice of cheese and the muffin lid.
4. Toast the muffin according to the manufacturer's instructions or until the bread is crisp and the cheese has melted. Serve immediately.

Baked Avocado Eggs

2 avocados, halved and stoned
4 medium eggs
1 tbsp parsley, finely chopped

1. Preheat the oven to 220°C (200°C fan) / 425F / gas 7.
2. Enlarge the stone cavity of the avocados with a teaspoon to make space for the eggs.
3. Arrange the avocados cut side up in a snug baking dish and break an egg into the middle of each one.
4. Season with salt and pepper, then bake for 18 minutes or until the egg whites have set, but the yolks are still a little runny.
5. Sprinkle with parsley and serve immediately.

SERVES: **6** | PREP TIME: **10 MINS** | COOKING TIME: **25 MINS**

BLT Waffle Sandwiches

250 g / 9 oz / 1 ⅔ cups plain (all purpose) flour
2 tsp baking powder
2 large eggs
300 ml / 10 ½ fl. oz / 1 ¼ cups milk
2 tbsp butter, melted
24 rashers smoked streaky bacon
6 lettuce leaves, halved
4 tomatoes, sliced

1. Put the oven on a low setting and put a non-stick electric waffle maker on to heat.
2. Mix the flour and baking powder in a bowl and make a well in the centre. Add the eggs and pour in the milk then use a whisk to gradually incorporate all of the flour from round the outside. Whisk in the butter.
3. Spoon some of the batter into the waffle maker and close the lid. Cook for 4 minutes or according to the manufacturer's instructions until golden brown. Repeat until all the batter has been used, keeping the finished batches warm in the oven.
4. Meanwhile, fry or grill the bacon until golden brown. When the waffles are ready, separate them into quarters and sandwich each pair of quarters together with bacon, lettuce and tomatoes. Serve immediately.

Main Meals

SERVES: 4 | **PREP TIME: 20 MINS** | **COOKING TIME: 40 MINS**

Chicken Fajita Bake

2 tbsp olive oil

1 onion, finely chopped

2 cloves of garlic, crushed

2 red chillies (chilies), finely chopped

400 g / 14 oz / 2 cups fresh or canned
    tomatoes, chopped

300 g / 10 ½ oz / 2 cups leftover cooked
    chicken, sliced

8 flour tortillas

100 g / 3 ½ oz / 1 cup Cheddar
    cheese, grated

1 handful parsley, chopped

1. Preheat the oven to 220°C (200°C fan)
   / 425F / gas 7.
2. Heat the oil in a saucepan and fry
   the onion for 5 minutes, stirring
   occasionally. Add the garlic and
   chillies and cook for 2 more minutes.
3. Add the tomatoes and a splash of
   water and simmer for 15 minutes.
4. Tip half of the tomato sauce into a
   bowl and set aside. Add the chicken
   to the saucepan and warm through.
5. Divide the chicken mixture between
   the tortillas and roll them up tightly.
   Arrange in a snug single layer in a
   baking dish. Pour the reserved
   tomato sauce over the top and
   scatter with cheese and parsley.
6. Bake in the oven for 15 minutes
   or until the cheese is fully melted
   and bubbling.

SERVES: 1 | PREP TIME: 5 MINS

Triple-decker Sandwich

4 slices wholemeal bread

1 tbsp soft goat's cheese

2 lettuce leaves

1 tsp mustard

4 slices wafer thin smoked ham

1 tbsp mayonnaise

6 slices cucumber

4 slices tomato

1. Spread one slice of the bread with goat's cheese and top with one of the lettuce leaves.
2. Add a second slice of bread and spread with mustard. Top with the ham.
3. Add a third slice of bread and spread with half of the mayonnaise. Top with cucumber and tomato, followed by the other lettuce leaf.
4. Spread the underside of the final slice of bread with the rest of the mayonnaise and lay it on top, then hold everything together with a wooden skewer.

Tomato Soup

2 tbsp olive oil

1 onion, finely chopped

3 cloves of garlic, crushed

400 g / 14 oz / 2 cups canned tomatoes, chopped

500 ml / 17 ½ fl. oz / 2 cups vegetable stock

1 tsp caster (superfine) sugar

Greek yogurt and fresh chives, to serve

1. Heat the oil in a saucepan and fry the onion for 8 minutes or until softened.
2. Add the garlic and cook for 2 more minutes, then stir in the tomatoes and vegetable stock and bring to the boil.
3. Simmer for 20 minutes then blend until smooth with a liquidizer or immersion blender.
4. Taste the soup and adjust the seasoning with sugar, salt and pepper.
5. Ladle into bowls and garnish with yogurt, chives and black pepper.

Cheesy Baked Mushrooms

4 portabella mushrooms, stalks removed

5 button mushrooms, stalks removed

2 tbsp olive oil

2 tbsp pesto

4 cherry tomatoes, quartered

125 g / 4 ½ oz / 1 ball mozzarella, chopped

2 tbsp Gruyere cheese, grated

2 tbsp flat leaf parsley, finely chopped, plus a few leaves to garnish

1. Preheat the oven to 200°C (180°C fan) / 400F / gas 6.
2. Brush the mushrooms with oil and arrange them open-side-up in a greaseproof paper lined baking dish.
3. Fill the portabella mushrooms with pesto and the button mushrooms with tomato. Mix the mozzarella with the Gruyere and parsley and sprinkle over the top.
4. Bake the mushrooms for 25 minutes or until tender to the point of a knife.
5. Season with black pepper and serve immediately.

SERVES: 1 | PREP TIME: **5 MINS** | COOKING TIME: **12 MINS**

Chicken and Avocado Salad

1 x 125 g / 4 ½ oz skinless chicken breast
2 tbsp olive oil
1 large handful mixed salad leaves
½ avocado, peeled and stoned
2 cherry tomatoes, halved
1 tbsp lemon juice
½ tsp caster (superfine) sugar
½ tsp mustard

1. Heat a griddle pan until smoking hot. Brush the chicken with 1 tablespoon of the oil and season all over with salt and pepper.
2. Griddle the chicken for 12 minutes, turning every 3 minutes, or until it's cooked through and nicely marked. Cut the chicken across into three big pieces.
3. Arrange the lettuce leaves in a bowl and top with the avocado, tomatoes and chicken.
4. Whisk the rest of the oil with the lemon juice, sugar and mustard and season with salt and pepper. Drizzle it over the salad and serve immediately.

Ham, Cheese and Salad Sandwiches

4 thick slices white bloomer

2 tbsp mayonnaise

2 lettuce leaves

1 tomato, sliced

4 slices smoked ham

6 slices cucumber

4 slices Emmental cheese

1 handful pea shoots

1. Heat a griddle pan until smoking hot, then toast the bread on one side until attractively marked.
2. Spread the untoasted side with mayonnaise and top two of the slices with lettuce, tomato, ham, cucumber, Emmental and pea shoots.
3. Put the other slices of bread on top, then cut in half and secure with cocktail sticks.

Steak and Salad Flatbreads

1 small rump steak

2 flatbreads

1 tsp mustard

1 ½ tbsp mayonnaise

4 little gem lettuce leaves

½ red pepper, sliced

2 spring onions (scallions), sliced

2 tbsp canned sweetcorn

1. Heat a frying pan until smoking hot. Season the steak generously with salt and pepper, then cook for 4 minutes on each side. Transfer to a plate and leave to rest while you assemble the flatbreads.
2. Warm the flatbreads in the frying pan for 20 seconds on each side.
3. Mix the mustard with the mayonnaise and spread thinly over the flatbreads. Top with lettuce, pepper, spring onion and sweetcorn.
4. Thinly slice the steak and divide between the flatbreads, then roll up and serve.

SERVES: **4** | PREP TIME: **10 MINS** | COOKING TIME: **30 MINS**

Spinach Soup

1 tbsp olive oil

2 tbsp butter

2 leeks, chopped

2 cloves of garlic, crushed

2 potatoes, peeled and diced

1 litre / 1 pint 15 fl. oz / 4 cups
   vegetable stock

¼ tsp nutmeg, freshly grated

200 g / 7 oz / 6 cups spinach, washed

Greek yogurt, to serve

1. Heat the oil and butter in a saucepan
   and fry the leeks for 8 minutes or
   until softened.
2. Add the garlic and potatoes to the
   pan and cook for 2 more minutes,
   then stir in the vegetable stock and
   bring to the boil.
3. Simmer for 15 minutes or until the
   potatoes are tender, then adjust the
   seasoning with nutmeg, salt and
   black pepper.
4. Stir the spinach into the pan, a couple
   of handfuls at a time, waiting for it
   to wilt down before adding the
   next batch.
5. As soon as it has all been incorporated,
   transfer the soup to a liquidizer and
   blend until very smooth.
6. Serve the soup in bowls with a
   dollop of yogurt on the top.

Penne with Mushrooms

400 g / 14 oz / 4 cups penne
75 ml / 2 ½ fl. oz / ⅓ cup olive oil
300 g / 10 ½ oz / 3 cups shimeji or baby
  chestnut mushrooms
2 cloves of garlic, crushed
100 ml / 3 ½ fl. oz / ½ cup dry white wine
100 g / 3 ½ oz / 1 cup Pecorino Romano or
  Parmesan, grated
2 handfuls rocket (arugula)

1. Boil the pasta in salted water according to the packet instructions or until al dente.
2. Meanwhile, heat the oil in a large sauté pan and fry the mushrooms for 8 minutes.
3. Add the garlic and stir-fry for 1 minute, then pour in the wine and bubble until reduced by half.
4. Drain the pasta and toss with the mushrooms. Divide between four warm bowls and scatter over the cheese and rocket.

Potato and Spinach Tortilla

75 ml / 2 ½ oz / ⅓ cup olive oil
1 onion, thinly sliced
50 g / 1 ¾ oz / 1 ½ cups baby leaf
  spinach, washed
4 small boiled potatoes, cooled and sliced
6 large eggs

1. Heat half the oil in a non-stick frying pan and fry the onion with a pinch of salt and pepper for 5 minutes. Add the spinach to the pan and cook until it has wilted and any liquid has evaporated.
2. Meanwhile, gently beat the eggs in a jug to break up the yolks.
3. When the spinach is ready, stir it into the eggs with the potatoes and season with salt and pepper.
4. Heat the rest of the oil in the frying pan then pour in the egg mixture.
5. Cook over a gentle heat for 6–8 minutes or until the egg has set round the outside, but the centre is still a bit soft.
6. Turn it out onto a plate, then slide it back into the pan and cook the other side for 4–6 minutes.
7. Leave to cool for 5 minutes before serving.

SERVES: **1** | PREP TIME: **10 MINS** | COOKING TIME: **10 MINS**

Cheese and Steak Panini

1 thin minute steak
2 tbsp olive oil
½ small onion, thinly sliced
½ green pepper, thinly sliced
1 focaccia roll, halved horizontally
2 slices Provolone cheese

1. Lay the steak between two sheets of clingfilm and use a rolling pin or wine bottle to gently bash it out to 3 mm thick. Cut into sections to make it easier to fry.
2. Heat a frying pan until smoking hot. Brush the steak with half of the oil and season with salt and pepper. Fry for 30 seconds on each side, then transfer to a plate.
3. Reduce the heat of the frying pan and add the rest of the oil with the onion and green pepper. Stir-fry for 5 minutes.
4. Preheat a panini press or sandwich toaster. Arrange the steak on the base of the roll and top with the peppers and onions. Lay the cheese on top and cover with the roll lids.
5. Toast the sandwich for 3 minutes or until the bread is golden brown and the cheese has melted. Cut in half and serve immediately.

Fusilli Pasta Salad

400 g / 14 oz / 4 cups fusilli
50 ml / 1 ¾ fl. oz / ¼ cup olive oil
1 lemon, juiced
150 g / 5 ½ oz / ⅔ cup sundried tomatoes in oil
100 g / 3 ½ oz / ½ cup capers in brine, drained
2 large handfuls mixed salad leaves
2 tbsp pine nuts, toasted
30 g Parmesan

1. Boil the pasta in salted water according to the packet instructions or until al dente.
2. Drain the pasta, then plunge into iced water to cool. Drain well.
3. Toss the pasta with the rest of the ingredients, except for the Parmesan and season to taste with salt and pepper.
4. Use a vegetable peeler to shave over the Parmesan just before serving.

SERVES: **6** | PREP TIME: **5 MINS** | COOKING TIME: **40 MINS**

Baked Potatoes with Chilli Con Carne

2 tbsp olive oil
1 onion, finely chopped
2 cloves of garlic, crushed
½ tsp cayenne pepper
450 g / 1 lb / 3 cups minced beef
400 g / 14 oz / 2 cups canned tomatoes, chopped
200 ml / 7 fl. oz / ¾ cup beef stock
400 g / 14 oz / 2 cups canned kidney beans, drained
6 baking potatoes
100 ml / 3 ½ fl. oz / ½ cup soured cream
100 g / 3 ½ oz / 1 cup Double Gloucester cheese, grated
4 spring onions (scallions), chopped

1. Preheat the oven to 220°C (200°C fan) / 425F / gas 7.
2. Heat the oil in a large saucepan and fry the onion for 5 minutes, stirring occasionally. Add the garlic and cayenne and cook for 2 minutes, then add the mince.
3. Fry the mince until it starts to brown then add the chopped tomatoes, stock and kidney beans and bring to a gentle simmer. Cook the chilli con carne for 30 minutes, stirring occasionally, until the mince is tender and the sauce has thickened a little.
4. Meanwhile, prick the potatoes and microwave for 5 minutes. Transfer the potatoes to the oven a bake for 30 minutes.
5. Taste the chilli for seasoning and add salt and freshly ground black pepper as necessary. Cut open the potatoes and fill with chilli con carne. Add a dollop of soured cream to each one and sprinkle with cheese and spring onions before serving.

SERVES: 6 | PREP TIME: 5 MINS | COOKING TIME: 40 MINS

Vegetarian Chilli

2 tbsp olive oil

1 onion, finely chopped

2 cloves of garlic, crushed

½ tsp cayenne pepper

450 g / 1 lb / 3 cups veggie mince

400 g / 14 oz / 2 cups canned tomatoes, chopped

200 ml / 7 fl. oz / ¾ cup vegetable stock

400 g / 14 oz / 2 cups canned mixed beans, drained

200 g / 7 oz / 1 cup canned sweetcorn, drained

100 g / 3 ½ oz / 1 cup Double Gloucester cheese, grated

100 g / 3 ½ oz / 1 cup Cheddar, grated

2 tbsp coriander (cilantro), chopped

lime wedges and tortilla chips to serve

1. Heat the oil in a large saucepan and fry the onion for 5 minutes, stirring occasionally. Add the garlic and cayenne and cook for 2 minutes, then add the mince.

2. Fry the mince until it starts to brown then add the chopped tomatoes, stock, beans and sweetcorn and bring to a gentle simmer. Cook for 30 minutes, stirring occasionally, until the mince is tender and the sauce has thickened a little.

3. Season to taste with salt and pepper.

4. Divide the chilli between six warm bowls. Mix the two cheeses together and sprinkle on top with the parsley, then serve with lime wedges and tortilla chips on the side.

Macaroni Cheese

400 g / 14 oz / 4 cups dried macaroni
2 tbsp butter
2 tbsp plain (all-purpose) flour
600 ml / 1 pint / 2 ½ cups milk
150 g / 5 ½ oz / 1 ½ cup Cheddar
  cheese, grated
2 tbsp dried breadcrumbs

1. Preheat the oven to 180°C (160°C fan) / 350F / gas 4.
2. Cook the macaroni in boiling, salted water for 10 minutes or until almost cooked. Drain well.
3. Meanwhile, put the butter, flour and milk in a saucepan. Cook the sauce over a low heat, stirring constantly, until the mixture bubbles and thickens. Take the pan off the heat and stir in two thirds of the cheese. Season to taste with salt and pepper.
4. Stir the macaroni into the cheese sauce and scrape it into a baking dish.
5. Sprinkle over the remaining cheese and the breadcrumbs, then bake for 30 minutes or until the top is golden brown and the pasta is cooked.

Easy Focaccia Pizza

1 oval focaccia
2 tbsp tomato pizza sauce
150 g / 5 ½ oz / 1 cup mini mozzarella
  balls, halved
8 cherry tomatoes, halved
½ tsp dried oregano
1 handful basil leaves

1. Preheat the oven to 200°C (180°C fan) / 400F / gas 6.
2. Lay the focaccia on a baking tray and spread with tomato pizza sauce.
3. Top with mozzarella and tomatoes, then scatter with oregano and basil leaves.
4. Bake the pizza for 10 minutes or until the cheese has melted and the tomatoes are soft.
5. Cut into slices and serve immediately.

SERVES: **4** | PREP TIME: **5 MINS** | COOKING TIME: **20 MINS**

Tagliatelle with Tomato and Prawns

3 tbsp olive oil

1 small onion, finely chopped

2 cloves of garlic, crushed

½ tsp chilli (chili) flakes

200 g / 7 oz / 1 cup canned chopped tomatoes

400 g / 14 oz dried tagliatelle

24 raw king prawns, peeled with tails left intact

a handful of basil leaves, chopped

1. Heat the oil in a sauté pan and fry the shallot, garlic and chilli flakes for 5 minutes. Stir in the tomatoes and cook over a low heat for 15 minutes, stirring occasionally. Season to taste with salt and pepper.
2. Meanwhile, cook the pasta in boiling, salted water according to the packet instructions or until al dente.
3. Towards the end of the pasta cooking time, add the prawns to the tomato sauce and cook until the underneath turns pink. Turn them over and cook until pink on the other side.
4. Drain the pasta and divide between four warm bowls. Spoon over the sauce and scatter with basil before serving.

SERVES: **4** | PREP TIME: **5 MINS** | COOKING TIME: **5 MINS**

Forager's Vegetable Stew

2 tbsp olive oil

1 onion, finely chopped

1 celery stick, finely chopped

1 carrot, cubed

150 g / 5 ½ oz / ¾ cup pearl barley

1 litre / 1 pint 15 fl. oz / 4 cups vegetable stock

2 large potatoes, peeled and cubed

30 g / 1 oz / 1 cup stinging nettles, picked with gloves and chopped

30 g / 1 oz / 1 cup ransom (wild garlic), chopped

wholemeal bread, to serve

1. Heat the oil in a large saucepan and gently fry the onion, celery and carrot for 5 minutes without colouring.
2. Stir in the barley then pour in the stock and bring to the boil.
3. Turn the heat down and simmer the stew for 25 minutes.
4. Add the potatoes and continue to simmer for 20 minutes or until the barley and potatoes are tender.
5. Add the nettles and ransom to the pan and simmer for 1 minute or until they just start to wilt, then season to taste with salt and pepper.
6. Ladle the stew into four bowls and serve with wholemeal bread.

MAKES: **2** | PREP TIME: **2 HOURS** | COOKING TIME: **12 MINS**

Pepperoni and Mushroom Pizza

200 g / 7 oz / 1 ⅓ cups strong white bread flour, plus extra for dusting

½ tsp easy blend dried yeast

2 tsp caster (superfine) sugar

1 tsp fine sea salt

1 tbsp olive oil

75 ml / 2 ½ fl. oz / ⅓ cup canned tomatoes, chopped

½ yellow pepper, sliced

½ red pepper, sliced

½ green pepper, sliced

1 handful pepperoni slices

2 slices ham, torn into small pieces

1 handful cherry tomatoes, halved

4 button mushrooms, sliced

1 red chilli, washed

3 sprigs of basil

1. Mix together the flour, yeast, sugar and salt and stir the oil into 140 ml of warm water. Stir the liquid into the dry ingredients then knead on a lightly oiled surface for 10 minutes or until smooth and elastic.

2. Leave the dough to rest covered with oiled clingfilm for 1- 2 hours until doubled in size.

3. Preheat the oven to 240°C (220°C fan) / 475F / gas 9 and grease two large baking trays.

4. Knead the dough for 2 more minutes then divide into two pieces. Roll them out into circles. Transfer the bases to the prepared trays and spread with the canned tomato.

5. Arrange the peppers, pepperoni, ham, cherry tomatoes, mushrooms and red chilli on top.

6. Bake for 12 minutes or until the bases are cooked through underneath.

7. Cut into quarters before serving.

Fishcakes with Dill

225 g / 8 oz / 1 ½ cups skinless, boneless
  pollock fillet, cubed
225 g / 8 oz / 1 ½ cups skinless boneless
  salmon fillet, cubed
100 g / 3 ½ oz / 1 ⅓ cups fresh
  white breadcrumbs
1 large egg, plus 1 egg yolk
1 small bunch dill, chopped
1 tsp Dijon mustard
2 tbsp plain (all-purpose) flour
2 tbsp sunflower oil

1. Put all of the ingredients, except for the flour, in a food processor with a pinch
   of salt and pepper and pulse until finely chopped and evenly mixed.
2. Flour your hands and shape the mixture into six patties. Chill in the fridge for at
   least 1 hour.
3. Heat the oil in a frying pan. Depending on the size of the pan, you may need to
   cook the fishcakes in batches. Fry the fishcakes over a medium-low heat for
   3 minutes on each side or until cooked through. Serve immediately.

Beef with
Spring Onion

1 small head broccoli, broken into florets
2 tbsp sunflower oil
1 clove of garlic, chopped
1 tbsp fresh root ginger, chopped
4 spring onions (scallions), chopped and
  green and white parts separated
1 large sirloin steak, thinly sliced
60 ml / 2 fl. oz / ¼ cup oyster sauce
steamed rice to serve

1. Boil or steam the broccoli for 3 minutes or until tender, then drain and set aside.
2. Heat the oil in a large wok and fry the garlic, ginger and spring onion whites
   for 1 minute.
3. Add the steak and stir-fry for 3 minutes or until it starts to colour.
4. Pour in the oyster sauce, adding a splash of water if the sauce is too thick.
   Stir-fry for 1 minute, then toss with the broccoli and spring onion greens.
5. Serve immediately on a bed of steamed rice.

SERVES: 4 | PREP TIME: 15 MINS | COOKING TIME: 10 MINS

Pad Thai

200 g / 7 oz dried Pho or Pad Thai rice noodles

3 tbsp vegetable oil

2 large eggs, beaten

2 cloves garlic, finely chopped

1 tbsp root ginger, julienned

3 spring onions (scallions), chopped

200 g / 7 oz / 1 ⅓ cups raw prawns, peeled with tails left intact

2 tbsp oyster sauce

1 tbsp light soy sauce

2 limes, 1 juiced, 1 cut into 8 pieces

2 tsp caster (superfine) sugar

3 tbsp salted peanuts, finely chopped

1 tsp chilli flakes

sliced chilli and parsley leaves to garnish

1. Put the rice noodles into a heatproof bowl, cover with boiling water and leave to soften for 15 minutes.
2. Heat half the oil in a large wok then pour in the egg. Cook for 1 minute or until almost set, then flip it over and cook the other side. Slide it onto a chopping board and cut into small pieces.
3. Add the rest of the oil to the wok and fry the garlic, ginger and spring onions for 30 seconds.
4. Add the prawns and stir fry for 2 minutes or until they just turn opaque.
5. Stir the oyster sauce, soy, lime juice and sugar together and add it to the wok, followed by the drained noodles.
6. Stir-fry for 1 more minute then stir in the peanuts and divide between four warm bowls.
7. Top each bowl with a couple of chunks of lime and a sprinkle of chilli flakes, then garnish with chilli and parsley.

Aubergine and Halloumi Burgers

1 small aubergine (eggplant), cut into 4 mm slices

2 small courgettes (zucchini), cut lengthways into 4 mm slices

50 ml / 1 ¾ fl. oz / ¼ cup olive oil

4 sesame burger buns, halved horizontally

250 g / 9 oz / 1 block halloumi, cut horizontally into 4 slices

2 tbsp mayonnaise

4 lettuce leaves

1. Lay the aubergine and courgette slices out on a clean work surface and season on both sides with salt and pepper. Leave to sweat for 15 minutes, then blot dry thoroughly with kitchen paper.
2. Heat a couple of griddle pans until smoking hot and brush the vegetables with olive oil. Cook in batches for 2 minutes on each side or until the vegetables are pleasingly marked. Keep warm in a low oven.
3. Toast the cut side of the burger buns on the griddle and set aside, then griddle the halloumi slices.
4. Spread the buns with mayonnaise and top the bases with lettuce before layering up the vegetables and halloumi. Put on the bun lids and serve immediately.

SERVES: **4** | PREP TIME: **5 MINS** | COOKING TIME: **50 MINS**

Lentil Stew

50 ml / 1 ¾ fl. oz / ¼ cup olive oil

2 leeks, sliced

4 small carrots, cut into chunks

2 cloves of garlic, sliced

1 tbsp tomato puree

1 litre / 1 pint 15 fl. oz / 4 cups vegetable stock

400 g / 14 oz / 3 ¼ cups green lentils

2 bay leaves

mint sprigs, to garnish

1. Heat the oil in a large saucepan and fry the leeks, carrots and garlic for 5 minutes.
2. Stir in the tomato puree, stock, lentils and bay leaves then simmer for 45 minutes or until the lentils are tender. If the liquid evaporates too quickly, add a little boiling water.
3. Taste for seasoning and add salt and black pepper as necessary then discard the bay leaves.
4. Divide between four warm bowls and serve garnished with mint.

Creamy Mushroom Tagliatelle

2 tbsp olive oil

1 tbsp butter

200 g / 7 oz / 2 ⅔ cups mushrooms, sliced

1 tbsp rosemary

1 tbsp thyme

2 cloves of garlic, finely chopped

200 ml / 7 fl. oz / ¾ cup double cream

200 g / 7 oz / 2 cups tagliatelle

50 g / 1 ¾ oz / ½ cup Parmesan, finely grated

1. Heat the oil and butter in a sauté pan and fry the mushrooms, rosemary and thyme for 10 minutes or until any liquid from the mushrooms evaporates and they start to colour.
2. Add the garlic and cook for 2 more minutes, stirring all the time, then add the cream and bring to a gentle simmer.
3. While the sauce is cooking, boil the tagliatelle in salted water according to the packet instructions or until al dente. Drain well.
4. Stir the Parmesan into the sauce, then toss with the tagliatelle and divide between two warm plates.

Blue Cheese Risotto

1 litre / 1 pint 15 fl. oz / 4 cups vegetable stock

2 tbsp olive oil

1 onion, finely chopped

2 cloves of garlic, crushed

150 g / 5 ½ oz / ¾ cup risotto rice

2 tbsp butter

150 g / 5 ½ oz / 1 cup blue cheese, diced

1 handful basil leaves

1. Heat the stock in a saucepan and keep it just below simmering point.
2. Heat the olive oil in a sauté pan and gently fry the onion for 5 minutes without colouring. Add the garlic and cook for 2 more minutes then stir in the rice.
3. When it is well coated with the oil, add two ladles of the hot stock.
4. Cook, stirring occasionally, until most of the stock has been absorbed before adding the next two ladles. Continue in this way for around 20 minutes or until the rice is just tender.
5. Stir in the butter, then cover the pan and take off the heat to rest for 4 minutes.
6. Fold through the blue cheese and half of the basil, then season to taste with salt and pepper. Divide between two warm bowls, scatter over the rest of the basil and serve immediately.

SERVES: **6** | PREP TIME: **1 HOUR** | COOKING TIME: **40 MINS**

Leek and Mushroom Quiche

2 tbsp butter

1 large leek, thinly sliced

2 cloves of garlic, sliced

225 g / 8 oz / 3 cups mixed mushrooms, chopped

3 large eggs, beaten

225 ml / 8 fl. oz / ¾ cup double (heavy)cream

75 g / 2 ½ oz / ½ cup Gruyere, grated

basil and parsley, to garnish

FOR THE PASTRY

110 g / 4 oz / ½ cup butter, cubed and chilled

225 g / 8 oz / 1 ½ cups plain (all-purpose) flour

1. To make the pastry, rub the butter into the flour until the mixture resembles fine breadcrumbs. Stir in just enough cold water to bring the pastry together into a pliable dough, then chill for 30 minutes.

2. Preheat the oven to 200°C (180°C fan) / 400F / gas 6.

3. Roll out the pastry and use it to line a 23 cm (9 in) loose-bottomed tart tin. Prick it with a fork, line with clingfilm and fill with baking beans. Bake for 10 minutes, then remove the clingfilm and beans and cook for 5 minutes or until crisp.

4. Lower the oven to 150°C (130°C fan) / 300F / gas 2. Heat the butter in a large sauté pan and fry the leeks for 5 minutes. Add the garlic and mushrooms and sauté for 10 minutes.

5. Whisk the eggs with the double cream then stir in the mushroom mixture. Season generously with salt and pepper.

6. Pour the filling into the pastry case and scatter the cheese on top.

7. Bake for 40 minutes or until just set in the centre. Leave the quiche to cool to room temperature, then garnish with basil and parsley and serve.

SERVES: **4** | PREP TIME: **1 HOUR 45 MINS** | COOKING TIME: **20 MINS**

Chicken Dippers and Chips

4 large Maris Piper potatoes, peeled and cut into skinny chips

200 g / 7 oz / 1 ⅓ cups plain (all purpose)

2 tbsp olive oil

250 ml / 9 fl. oz / 1 cup pale ale

4 skinless chicken breasts, sliced lengthways

sunflower oil for deep-frying

mayonnaise, to serve

1. Soak the potatoes in cold water for 1 hour to reduce the starch.
2. Drain the chips and dry completely with a clean tea towel, then air-dry on a wire rack for 30 minutes.
3. Meanwhile, make the batter. Sieve the flour into a bowl then whisk in the oil and ale until smoothly combined.
4. Heat the oil in a deep fat fryer, according to the manufacturer's instructions, to a temperature of 130°C (265F). Par-cook the chips for 10 minutes so that they cook all the way through but don't brown. Drain the chips on plenty of kitchen paper to absorb the excess oil.
5. Increase the fryer temperature to 180°C (350F). Dip the chicken in the batter and fry for 6 minutes or until golden brown. Transfer the chicken to a kitchen paper lined bowl and increase the fryer temperature to 190°C (375F).
6. Return the chips to the fryer basket and cook for 4 minutes or until crisp and golden brown. Drain the chips of excess oil and serve straight away with the chicken and some mayonnaise for dipping.

MAKES: **1** | PREP TIME: **2 HOUR** | COOKING TIME: **12 MINS**

Pepperoni, Olive and Onion Pizza

150 g / 5 ½ oz / 1 cup strong white bread flour, plus extra for dusting
½ tsp easy blend dried yeast
½ tsp fine sea salt
½ tbsp olive oil
2 tbsp tomato pizza sauce
125 g / 4 ½ oz / 1 ball mozzarella, sliced
10 slices pepperoni
¼ red onion, sliced
4 black olives, stoned and sliced
¼ tsp herbes de Provence

1. Mix together the flour, yeast and salt and stir the oil into 100 ml of warm water.
   Stir the liquid into the dry ingredients then knead on a lightly oiled surface for
   10 minutes or until smooth and elastic.
2. Leave the dough to rest covered with oiled clingfilm for 1–2 hours until doubled
   in size.
3. Preheat the oven to 240°C (220°C fan) / 475F / gas 9 and grease a large baking tray.
4. Knead the dough for 2 more minutes then roll it out into a rough circle.
5. Transfer the base to the prepared tray and spread with tomato pizza sauce.
6. Arrange the cheese, pepperoni, onion and olives on top and sprinkle with herbes
   de Provence.
7. Bake for 12 minutes or until the base is cooked through underneath.
8. Serve immediately.

Salmon and Vegetable Bake

2 thick salmon steaks
175 g / 6 oz / 1 ½ cups broccoli, broken
  into small florets
200 g / 7 oz / 1 ⅔ cups baby sprouts
6 cherry tomatoes
3 small shallots, cut into wedges
½ lemon
2 sprigs rosemary
50 ml / 1 ¾ fl. oz / ¼ cup olive oil
1 tbsp fresh thyme, chopped
½ tsp mixed peppercorns, crushed

1. Preheat the oven to 200°C (180°C fan) / 400F / gas 6.
2. Arrange the salmon steaks in a baking dish and surround with the broccoli,
   sprouts, tomatoes and shallots.
3. Cut a slice from the lemon, then cut it in half and use to garnish the salmon with
   the rosemary. Squeeze the rest of the lemon half, then whisk in the oil, thyme,
   peppercorns and ½ tsp salt.
4. Drizzle the mixture all over the salmon and vegetables, then bake for 25 minutes
   or until the fish is just cooked in the centre and the vegetables are tender.

Tagliatelle with Chicken and Pesto

½ clove of garlic
1 ½ tbsp pine nuts, toasted
50 g / 1 ¾ oz / 2 cups basil leaves,
  plus extra to garnish
25 g Pecorino, finely grated
200 ml / 7 fl. oz / ¾ cup extra virgin olive oil
2 skinless chicken breasts, sliced
500 g / 1 lb 1 ¾ oz fresh egg tagliatelle

1. Crush the garlic with a pinch of salt in a large pestle and mortar until well pulped.
   Add the pine nuts and pound until broken up but not pasty.
2. Add the basil a handful at a time and pound until well pulped then stir in the
   cheese and all but 2 tbsp of the olive oil.
3. Heat the remaining 2 tbsp olive oil in a frying pan and season the chicken with salt
   and pepper. Fry the chicken over a medium heat for 5 minutes or until cooked
   through and golden brown.
4. Meanwhile, cook the tagliatelle in boiling water for 3 minutes or until al dente,
   then drain well and toss with the pesto and chicken.
5. Divide between four warm bowls and serve immediately, garnished with basil.

SERVES: 4 | **PREP TIME: 5 MINS** | **COOKING TIME: 45 MINS**

Chicken Curry

2 tbsp sunflower oil

1 onion, finely chopped

1 tbsp fresh root ginger, grated

3 cloves of garlic, crushed

8 skinless, boneless chicken thighs, cut into chunks

1 tbsp curry powder

400 g / 14 oz / 2 cups canned tomatoes, chopped

200 ml/ 7 fl. oz / ¾ cup coconut milk

2 tbsp mango chutney

1 small bunch coriander, chopped

1. Heat the oil in a large saucepan and fry the onion for 8 minutes stirring occasionally.

2. Add the ginger and garlic and stir-fry for 2 minutes.

3. Add the chicken and cook for 4 minutes, stirring occasionally, until it starts to colour on the outside, then sprinkle over the curry powder and continue to cook for 1 minute.

4. Add the chopped tomatoes, coconut milk and mango chutney and bring to a gentle simmer. If the sauce doesn't cover the chicken, add a little water.

5. Cook the curry for 30 minutes, stirring occasionally, until the chicken is tender and the sauce has thickened.

SERVES: 4 | PREP TIME: 5 MINS | COOKING TIME: 35 MINS

Squash and Chickpea Stew

50 ml / 1 ¾ fl. oz / ¼ cup olive oil

1 onion, finely chopped

1 celery stick, finely chopped

2 carrots, diced

2 cloves of garlic, finely chopped

1 tsp ground cumin

1 tsp smoked paprika

2 acorn squashes, peeled, deseeded and diced (or 1 small butternut squash)

400 g / 14 oz / 2 cups canned tomatoes, chopped

500 ml / 17 ½ fl. oz / 2 cups vegetable stock

50 g / 1 ¾ oz / ¼ cup mixed brown and wild rice

400 g / 14 oz / 2 cups canned chickpeas (garbanzo beans), drained

chives, to garnish

1. Heat the oil in a large saucepan and fry the onion, celery, carrot and garlic for 5 minutes to soften without colouring.
2. Add the spices and squash to the pan and stir to coat in the oil, then add the tomatoes, stock, rice and chickpeas.
3. Simmer for 25 minutes or until the squash and rice are tender.
4. Season to taste with salt and pepper, then ladle into four warm bowls and serve garnished with chives.

Chicken and Pork Meatballs with Linguini

75 ml / 2 ½ fl. oz / ⅓ cup olive oil
1 onion, finely chopped
1 clove of garlic, crushed
250 g / 9 oz / 1 ⅔ cups minced chicken
250 g / 9 oz 1 ⅔ cups sausagemeat
50 g / 1 ¾ oz / ⅔ cup fresh white breadcrumbs
2 tbsp basil leaves, chopped, plus extra to garnish
2 tbsp Parmesan, finely grated, plus extra to garnish
1 egg yolk
300 g / 10 ½ oz / 2 cups cherry tomatoes
400 g / 14 oz linguini

1. Preheat the oven to 200°C (180°C fan) / 400F / gas 6 and grease a baking dish.
2. Heat half of the oil in a frying pan and fry the onion for 5 minutes or until softened. Add the garlic and cook for 2 more minutes, stirring constantly, then scrape the mixture into a mixing bowl and leave to cool.
3. Add the chicken mince, sausagemeat, breadcrumbs, basil, Parmesan and egg yolk. Season with salt and pepper, then mix well and shape into 16 meatballs.
4. Mingle the meatballs and tomatoes in the baking dish and drizzle with the rest of the oil. Bake for 20 minutes or until the meatballs are cooked through and the tomatoes have burst.
5. Meanwhile, boil the pasta in salted water according to the packet instructions or until al dente. Drain the pasta and divide between four warm bowls.
6. Spoon over the meatballs and tomatoes and garnish with Parmesan and basil.

Tandoori Chicken Skewers

50 ml / 1 ¾ fl. oz / ¼ cup natural yogurt

1 clove of garlic, crushed

1 tsp curry powder

2 tsp mango chutney

4 skinless, boneless chicken thighs, cut
  into large chunks

2 tbsp coriander (cilantro) leaves, chopped

lemon wedges, to serve

1. Mix the yogurt with the garlic, curry powder and chutney and massage it into the chicken.
2. Leave to marinate for at least 1 hour in the fridge.
3. Preheat the grill to its highest setting. Thread the chicken pieces onto six metal skewers.
4. Cook the skewers under the grill for 4 minutes on each side, or until the chicken is cooked through.
5. Sprinkle with coriander and serve immediately with lemon wedges for squeezing over.

Homemade Burgers

450 g / 1 lb / 2 cups minced beef,
  not too lean

2 tbsp double cream

1 tsp Dijon mustard

2 tbsp sunflower oil

4 seeded burger buns, halved horizontally

2 tbsp mayonnaise

½ red onion, sliced

4 gherkins, sliced

50 g / 1 ¾ oz / 1 ½ cups mixed salad leaves

1 large tomato, sliced

1. Mix the mince with the cream and mustard and season generously with salt and pepper, then knead lightly until sticky. Divide the mixture into four and compress each one into a tight patty with your hands.
2. Heat the oil in a frying pan then fry the burgers for 8 minutes, turning every 2 minutes.
3. Spread the bun bases with mayonnaise and top with sliced onion.
4. Sit the burgers on top when they're ready and garnish with gherkin, salad leaves and tomato before adding the bun lids.

SERVES: 4 | **PREP TIME: 5 MINS** | **COOKING TIME: 30 MINS**

Courgette and Dill Frittata

4 tbsp olive oil

2 shallots, thinly sliced

2 courgettes (zucchini), halved and thinly sliced

1 garlic clove, crushed

6 large eggs

1 small bunch dill, finely chopped

1. Heat 3 tablespoons of the oil in an oven-proof frying pan and fry the shallot and courgette for 15 minutes over a low heat until softened and lightly caramelised. Add the garlic and season with salt and pepper then cook for 2 more minutes.

2. Preheat the grill to its highest setting. Gently beat the eggs in a jug to break up the yolks then stir in the courgette mixture and dill.

3. Wipe out the frying pan with kitchen paper then heat the rest of the oil in the pan. Pour in the egg mixture and cook over a gentle heat for 6-8 minutes or until the egg has set round the outside.

4. Put the frying pan under the grill to cook the top for 3-4 minutes or until golden brown and just set.

5. Slide the frittata onto a serving plate and leave to cool for a few minutes before serving.

Desserts

MAKES: 12 | **PREP TIME: 45 MINS** | **COOKING TIME: 15 MINS**

Black Forest Cupcakes

110 g / 4 oz / ⅔ cup self-raising
  flour, sifted

2 tbsp unsweetened cocoa powder

110 g / 4 oz / ½ cup caster
  (superfine) sugar

110 g / 4 oz / ½ cup butter, softened

2 large eggs

1 tsp almond extract

200 g / 7 oz / ⅔ cup cherry jam (jelly)

TO DECORATE

300 ml / 10 ½ fl. oz / 1 ¼ cup double
  (heavy) cream

12 cherries

2 tbsp milk chocolate flakes

1. Preheat the oven to 190°C (170°C fan)
   / 375F / gas 5 and line a 12-hole
   cupcake tin with paper cases.
2. Combine the flour, cocoa, sugar,
   butter, eggs and almond extract in a
   bowl and whisk together for 2 minutes
   or until smooth.
3. Divide half the mixture between the
   cases and add a big spoonful of jam
   to each one.
4. Top with the rest of the cake mixture,
   then transfer the tin to the oven and
   bake for 15 minutes or until a skewer
   inserted comes out clean.
5. Transfer the cakes to a wire rack and
   leave to cool completely.
6. Whisk the cream until it holds its
   shape, then spoon or pipe it onto the
   cakes. Top each one with a cherry and
   sprinkle with chocolate flakes.
7. These cupcakes will keep for
   several days in an air-tight container.

SERVES: **4** | PREP TIME: **20 MINS** | COOKING TIME: **1 MIN** | CHILLING: **1 HOUR**

Strawberry Verrines

135 g / 5 oz / ⅔ cup jelly strawberry (jello) cubes
150 g / 5 ½ oz / 1 cup strawberries, halved
2 tbsp runny honey
1 tsp vanilla extract
500 ml / 17 ½ fl. oz / 2 cups Greek yogurt

1. Put the jelly cubes in a microwaveable jug with 100 ml water and microwave on high for 1 minute. Stir to dissolve, then make up to 570 ml with cold water.
2. Stir in the strawberries and set aside.
3. Stir the honey and vanilla into the yogurt and divide a third of the mixture between four glasses.
4. Spoon over a third of the strawberries and half of the jelly liquid, then transfer to the fridge to set for 30 minutes.
5. Spoon another third of the yogurt on top and add a third of the strawberries and the rest of the jelly liquid, then return to the fridge for 30 minutes.
6. Top with the rest of the yogurt and the reserved strawberries and refrigerate until ready to serve.

MAKES: 2 | PREP TIME: 15 MINS | COOKING TIME: 2 MINS

Indulgent Mug Cakes

55 g / 2 oz / ¼ cup butter, softened
55 g / 2 oz / ¼ cup caster (superfine) sugar
1 large egg
55 g / 2 oz / ⅓ cup self-raising flour, sifted
1 tbsp cocoa powder
50 g / 1 ¾ oz / ⅓ cup dark chocolate (minimum 60% cocoa solids), chopped
2 tbsp double (heavy) cream
1 tbsp dark and white chocolate chips

1. Beat the butter and sugar together in a mug until pale and smooth.
2. Break the egg into a second mug and beat gently with a fork, then gradually stir the egg into the butter mixture.
3. Fold in the flour and cocoa powder, followed by 1 tablespoon of the chopped chocolate, then spoon half of the mixture into the mug you used to beat the egg and level the tops.
4. Transfer the mugs to a microwave and cook on full power for 1 minute 30 seconds. Test the cakes by inserting a skewer into the centre – if it comes out clean, they are ready. If not, return to the microwave for 15 seconds and test again.
5. In a separate mug, put the rest of the chopped chocolate and the cream.
6. Cook on medium power for 20 seconds and stir, then return to the microwave, checking every 10 seconds until the chocolate has melted. Stir until smooth, then drizzle over the cakes and decorate with chocolate chips.

MAKES: 9 | PREP TIME: 2 HOURS 30 MINS | COOKING TIME: 35 MINS

Apple and Cinnamon Rolls

400 g / 14 oz / 2 ⅔ cups strong white
  bread flour
½ tsp easy blend dried yeast
4 tbsp caster (superfine) sugar
1 tsp fine sea salt
1 tbsp olive oil
75 g / 2 ½ oz / ½ cup light brown sugar
1 ½ tsp ground cinnamon
25 g butter, softened
1 eating apple, peeled,
  cored and chopped
1 egg, beaten

1. Combine the flour, yeast, caster
   sugar and salt. Stir the oil into
   280 ml of warm water then stir it into
   the dry ingredients. Knead the dough
   on an oiled surface for 10 minutes or
   until smooth and elastic.
2. Leave the dough to rest in a lightly
   oiled bowl, covered with oiled
   clingfilm, for 1-2 hours or until
   doubled in size. Knead the dough
   for 2 more minutes, then roll out into
   a large rectangle.
3. Cream the brown sugar, cinnamon
   and butter together. Spread the
   mixture over the dough, then scatter
   over the apple and roll it up tightly.
   Cut the roll into nine even slices and
   arrange them in a round cake tin or
   ovenproof frying pan.
4. Cover the rolls with oiled clingfilm
   and leave to prove for 1 hour or until
   doubled in size.
5. Preheat the oven to 220°C (200°C fan)
   / 425F / gas 7.
6. Brush the rolls with egg then transfer
   the tray to the top shelf of the oven
   and bake for 35 minutes or until
   cooked through.

Individual Apple Crumbles

2 large bramley apple, peeled, cored
and chopped

2 tbsp caster (superfine) sugar

75 g / 2 ½ oz / ⅓ cup butter

100 g / 3 ½ oz / ⅔ cup plain
(all purpose) flour

25 g ground almonds

40 g light brown sugar

1. Preheat the oven to 180°C (160°C fan) / 350F / gas 4.
2. Mix the apples with the sugar and divide between six individual baking dishes
   or large ramekins.
3. Rub the butter into the flour and stir in the ground almonds and brown sugar.
   Squeeze a handful of the mixture into a clump and then crumble it over the fruit.
   Use up the rest of the topping in the same way, then shake the dishes to level
   the tops.
4. Bake the crumbles for 30 minutes or until the topping is golden brown and
   the fruit is bubbling.

Tiramisu

600 ml / 1 pint / 2 ½ cups double cream

300 g / 10 ½ oz / 1 ⅓ cups mascarpone

4 tbsp icing (confectioner's) sugar

100 ml / 3 ½ fl. oz / ½ cup Marsala or
chocolate liqueur

100 ml / 3 ½ fl. oz / ½ cup strong filter
coffee, cooled

300 g / 10 ½ oz sponge fingers

unsweetened cocoa powder for dusting

1. Put the cream, mascarpone and sugar in a bowl with half of the Marsala and whip
   with an electric whisk until it holds its shape.
2. Mix the rest of the Marsala with the coffee. Dip half of the sponge fingers in the
   coffee mixture and divide between six glass mugs. Spoon half of the cream mixture
   over the top.
3. Dip the rest of the sponge fingers in the coffee and arrange on top.
4. Spoon over the rest of the cream mixture and dust with cocoa.
5. Chill in the fridge for at least 1 hour before serving.

SERVES: **4** | PREP TIME: **45 MINS** | COOKING TIME: **20 MINS**

Chocolate Mousse Crêpes

100 ml / 3 ½ fl. oz / ½ cup double (heavy) cream
100 g / 3 ½ oz / ⅔ cup milk chocolate, chopped
1 large egg white
2 tbsp caster (superfine) sugar
whipped cream, to serve

FOR THE CRÊPES
150 g / 5 ½ oz / 1 cup plain (all purpose) flour
1 large egg
325 ml / 11 ½ fl. oz / 1 ⅓ cups whole milk
1 tbsp butter

1. Heat the cream to simmering point then pour it over the chocolate and stir until smooth. Leave to cool for 10 minutes.
2. Whip the egg whites until stiff then whisk in the sugar. Stir a big spoonful of egg white into the cooled chocolate mixture then fold in the rest with a big metal spoon, keeping as many of the air bubbles intact as possible. Chill in the fridge while you make the pancakes.
3. Sieve the flour into a bowl and make a well in the centre. Break in the egg and pour in the milk then use a whisk to gradually incorporate all of the flour from around the outside.
4. Melt the butter in a small frying pan then whisk it into the batter. Put the buttered frying pan back over a low heat. Add a small ladle of batter and swirl the pan to coat the bottom.
5. When it starts to dry and curl up at the edges, turn the crepe over with a spatula and cook the other side until golden brown.
6. Repeat with the rest of the mixture then fill the crepes with three quarters of the chocolate mousse. Put the rest in a piping bag and pipe it over the top.
7. Serve with whipped cream.

Vanilla Cheesecake with Berries

200 g / 7 oz / 1 ⅓ cups shortbread, crushed
50 g / 1 ¾ oz / ¼ cup butter, melted
600 g / 1 lb 5 oz / 2 ¾ cups cream cheese
150 ml / 5 fl. oz / ⅔ cup soured cream
175 g / 6 oz / ¾ cup caster (superfine) sugar
2 large eggs, plus 1 egg yolk
2 tbsp plain (all purpose) flour
1 tsp vanilla extract
150 g / 5 ½ oz / 1 cup mixed berries
mint sprigs, to garnish

1. Preheat the oven to 180°C (160°C fan) / 350F / gas 4.
2. Grease a 23 cm (9 in) round loose-bottomed tart case.
3. Mix the biscuit crumbs with the butter and press into an even layer across the bottom and sides of the tin.
4. Whisk together the remaining ingredients, except for the berries and mint, until smooth.
5. Spoon the cheesecake mixture on top of the biscuit base and bake for 50 minutes or until the centre is only just set. Leave to cool completely in the tin.
6. Transfer the tin to the fridge and chill for 2 hours, then unmould and decorate with berries and mint.

MAKES: 12 | PREP TIME: 45 MINS | COOKING TIME: 20 MINS

Spiced Coffee and Walnut Muffins

1 large egg

120 ml / 4 fl. oz / ½ cup sunflower oil

120 ml / 4 fl. oz / ½ cup strong coffee, cooled

375 g / 12 ½ oz / 2 ½ cups self-raising flour, sifted

1 tsp baking powder

200 g / 7 oz / ¾ cup dark brown sugar

1 tsp ground cinnamon

½ tsp ground star anise

75 g / 2 ½ oz / ⅔ cup walnuts, chopped

300 ml / 10 ½ fl. oz / 1 ¼ cups double (heavy) cream

2 tbsp caramel sauce

1. Preheat the oven to 180°C (160°C fan) / 350F / gas 4 and line a 12-hole muffin tin with paper cases.
2. Beat the egg in a jug with the oil and coffee until well mixed.
3. Mix the flour, baking powder, sugar, spices and all but 2 tablespoons of the walnuts in a bowl. Pour in the egg mixture and stir just enough to combine.
4. Spoon the mixture into the cases, then bake in the oven for 20 minutes or until a skewer inserted comes out clean. Transfer the cakes to a wire rack and leave to cool completely.
5. Whip the cream until it holds its shape, then spoon it into a piping bag fitted with a large star nozzle. Pipe a big swirl on top of each cake.
6. Drizzle the muffins with caramel sauce and garnish with the reserved walnuts.
7. These muffins will keep for several days in an air-tight container.

SERVES: 8 | PREP TIME: 20 MINS | COOKING TIME: 35 MINS

Strawberry Sponge Cake

100 g / 3 ½ oz / ⅔ cups self-raising flour

100 g / 3 ½ oz / ½ cup caster (superfine) sugar

100 g / 3 ½ oz / ½ cup butter, softened

2 large eggs

1 tsp baking powder

1 tsp vanilla extract

100 g / 3 ½ oz / ⅔ cup strawberries, halved or quartered if large

icing (confectioner's) sugar for dusting

1. Preheat the oven to 180°C (160° fan) / 350F / gas 4 and grease a 20 cm (8in) round cake tin or ovenproof frying pan.
2. Put the flour, sugar, butter, eggs, baking powder and vanilla extract in a bowl and whisk with an electric whisk for 4 minutes or until pale and well whipped.
3. Fold in the strawberries, then scrape into the prepared tin and level the top with a spatula.
4. Bake for 35 minutes or until a skewer inserted comes out clean.
5. Transfer the cake to a wire rack and leave to cool completely.
6. Dust with icing sugar just before serving.
7. Delicious served with whipped cream.

MAKES: **12** | PREP TIME: **45 MINS** | COOKING TIME: **15 MINS**

Peppermint Cream Cupcakes

110 g / 4 oz / ⅔ cup self-raising flour, sifted
110 g / 4 oz / ½ cup caster (superfine) sugar
110 g / 4 oz / ½ cup butter, softened
2 large eggs
½ tsp peppermint extract
100 g / 3 ½ oz / ⅔ cup white chocolate chips

TO DECORATE
300 ml / 10 ½ fl. oz / 1 ¼ cup double (heavy) cream
50 g / 1 ¾ oz / ½ cup icing (confectioner's) sugar
½ tsp peppermint extract
mint sprigs, to garnish

1. Preheat the oven to 190°C (170°C fan) / 375F / gas 5 and line a 12-hole cupcake tin with paper cases.
2. Combine the flour, sugar, butter, eggs and peppermint extract in a bowl and whisk together for 2 minutes or until smooth. Fold in the chocolate chips then divide the mixture between the paper cases.
3. Bake for 15 minutes or until a skewer inserted comes out clean.
4. Transfer the cakes to a wire rack and leave to cool completely.
5. Whisk the cream with the icing sugar and peppermint extract until it holds its shape, then spoon into a piping bag fitted with a large star nozzle.
6. Pipe a big swirl onto each cake, then garnish with mint sprigs.
7. These cupcakes will keep for several days in an air-tight container.

MAKES: **6** | PREP TIME: **10 MINS** | COOKING TIME: **10 MINS** | CHILLING: **1 HOUR**

Fruity Chocolate Custards

450 ml / 12 ½ fl. oz / 1 ¾ cups whole milk

4 large egg yolks

75 g / 2 ½ oz / ⅓ cup caster (superfine) sugar

1 tsp cornflour (cornstarch)

2 tbsp unsweetened cocoa powder

150 g / 5 ½ oz / 1 cup mixed berries

mint sprigs, to garnish

1. Put the milk in a saucepan and bring to simmering point.
2. Whisk the egg yolks with the caster sugar, cornflour and cocoa until thick.
3. Gradually incorporate the hot milk, whisking all the time, then scrape the mixture back into the saucepan.
4. Stir the custard over a low heat until it thickens, then divide between six small ramekins.
5. Leave to cool, then chill in the fridge for 1 hour. Serve garnished with berries and mint.

Strawberry and Amaretti Creams

300 ml / 10 ½ fl. oz / 1 ¼ cups double (heavy) cream
2 tbsp icing (confectioner's) sugar
1 tsp vanilla extract
300 ml / 10 ½ fl. oz / 1 ¼ cups Greek yogurt
100 g / 3 ½ oz / 2 cups amaretti biscuits, crushed
150 g / 5 ½ oz / 1 cup strawberries, cut into quarters
50 ml / 1 ¾ fl. oz / ¼ cup amaretto liqueur

1. Whip the cream with the icing sugar and vanilla extract until it holds its shape, then fold in the yogurt.
2. Divide half of the mixture between six glasses and top with half of the biscuits and strawberries. Drizzle with half of the liqueur.
3. Repeat to make a second layer of the ingredients and serve immediately.

Blueberry Smoothie Lollies

225 g / 8 oz / 1 ½ cups blueberries
400 ml / 14 fl. oz / 1 ⅔ cups Greek yogurt
2 tbsp runny honey

1. Put all of the ingredients in a liquidizer and blend until smooth.
2. Divide between four disposable plastic cups and transfer to the freezer for 1 hour.
3. Insert a lolly stick into the centre of each one and freeze for a further 2 hours or until solid.
4. Dip the outside of each cup briefly in hot water to unmould before serving.

MAKES: 10 | PREP TIME: 25 MINS | COOKING TIME: 35 MINS

Choc-chip Blondies

100 g / 3 ½ oz / ⅔ cup white chocolate, chopped
225 g / 8 oz / 1 cup butter
450 g / 15 ½ oz light brown sugar
4 large eggs
100 g / 3 ½ oz / ⅔ cup self-raising flour
100 g / 3 ½ oz / ⅔ cup milk chocolate chips
75 g / 2 ½ oz / ⅔ cup almonds, chopped

1. Preheat the oven to 180°C (160°C fan) / 350F / gas 4 and oil and line a
   20 cm x 20 cm square cake tin.
2. Melt the white chocolate and butter together in a saucepan, then leave to cool
   a little.
3. Whisk together the sugar and eggs with an electric whisk for 3 minutes or until
   very light and creamy.
4. Pour in the chocolate mixture and sieve over the flour, then fold everything
   together with the chocolate chips and almonds until evenly mixed.
5. Scrape into the tin and bake for 35 minutes or until the outside is set, but the
   centre is still quite soft, as it will continue to cook as it cools.
6. Leave the blondie to cool completely before cutting into 10 pieces.
7. These blondies will keep for several days in an air-tight container.

SERVES: 8 | PREP TIME: 20 MINS | COOKING TIME: 45 MINS

Iced Lemon Drizzle Cake

150 g / 5 ½ oz / 1 cup self-raising flour

150 g / 5 ½ oz / ⅔ cup caster (superfine) sugar

150 g / 5 ½ oz / ⅔ cup butter, softened

3 large eggs

1 tsp baking powder

2 lemons, juiced zest finely grated

100 g / 3 ½ oz / ½ cup granulated sugar

FOR THE ICING

100 g / 3 ½ oz / ½ cup icing (confectioner's) sugar

1-2 tbsp lemon juice

4 slices crystallised lemon (optional)

1. Preheat the oven to 180°C (160°C fan) / 350F / gas 4 and grease and line a loaf tin with greaseproof paper.
2. Put the flour, caster sugar, butter, eggs, baking powder and lemon zest in a large mixing bowl and whisk with an electric whisk for 4 minutes or until pale and well whipped.
3. Scrape the mixture into the tin and level the top with a spatula.
4. Bake for 45 minutes or until a skewer inserted into the centre comes out clean.
5. While the cake is baking, stir the juice of the two lemons into the granulated sugar. As soon as the cake is ready, prick it with a skewer and spoon the syrup over the top.
6. Leave to cool completely.
7. Sieve the icing sugar into a bowl and add just enough lemon juice to make a thick glace icing. Spoon the icing over the cake and decorate with crystallised lemon slices.
8. This cake will keep for several days in an air-tight container.

MAKES: **9** | PREP TIME: **15 MINS** | COOKING TIME: **20 MINS**

Gluten-free Black Bean Brownies

50 g / 1 ¾ oz / ½ cup rolled porridge oats

2 tbsp unsweetened cocoa powder

1 tsp baking powder

400 g / 14 oz / 2 cups canned black beans, drained and rinsed

100 g / 3 ½ oz / ½ cup soft brown sugar

50 g / 1 ¾ oz / ¼ cup butter, melted

100 g / 3 ½ oz / ⅔ cup dark chocolate (min. 60 per cent cocoa solids), finely chopped

1. Preheat the oven to 180°C (160°C fan) / 350F / gas 4.
2. Oil and line a 20 cm (8 in) square cake tin with greaseproof paper.
3. Put the oats, cacao and baking powder in a food processor and blitz to a powder. Add the black beans, sugar, butter and chocolate and blend again until very smooth.
4. Scrape the mixture into the tin and level the top.
5. Bake for 20 minutes or until the outside is set, but the centre is still quite soft.
6. Leave the brownie to cool completely before cutting and serving.
7. These brownies will keep for several days in an air-tight container.

MAKES: **2** | PREP TIME: **10 MINS** | COOKING TIME: **1 HOUR 30 MINS**

Cookie Mug Cakes

55 g / 2 oz / ¼ cup butter, softened
55 g / 2 oz / ¼ cup caster (superfine) sugar
1 large egg
5 chocolate sandwich cookies
55 g / 2 oz / ⅓ cup self-raising flour, sifted

1. Beat the butter and sugar together in a large mug until pale and smooth.
2. Break the egg into a second mug and beat gently with a fork, then gradually stir the egg into the butter mixture.
3. Crumble four of the cookies and fold them in with the flour. Spoon half of the mixture into the mug you used to beat the egg and level the tops.
4. Transfer the mugs to a microwave and cook on full power for 1 minute 30 seconds. Test the cakes by inserting a skewer into the centre – if it comes out clean, they are ready. If not, return to the microwave for 15 seconds and test again.
5. Leave the cakes to cool for 5 minutes, then break the final cookie into pieces, arrange on top and serve.
6. Delicious served with whipped cream.

Summer Fruit Rice Pudding

110 g / 4 oz / ½ cup short grain rice

75 g / 2 ½ oz / ⅓ cup caster (superfine) sugar

1.2 litres / 2 pints / 4 ½ cups whole milk

1 tsp ground cinnamon

150 g / 5 ½ oz / 1 cup blueberries

1 nectarine, stoned and sliced

6 sprigs mint

1. Preheat the oven to 140°C (120°C fan) / 275F / gas 1.
2. Stir the rice and sugar into the milk in a baking dish, then cover and bake for 1 hour 30 minutes. Leave to stand for 30 minutes.
3. Divide the rice pudding between six bowls and sprinkle with cinnamon.
4. Top with blueberries, nectarine and mint. Serve warm or chilled.

Fig and Cashew Milkshake

3 fresh figs, chopped, plus extra to garnish

1 handful cashew nuts

250 ml / 9 fl. oz / 1 cup milk

1 tbsp runny honey

2 scoops vanilla ice cream

1. Put the figs, cashew nuts, milk and honey in a liquidizer and blend until smooth.
2. Add the ice cream and blend again for 10 seconds.
3. Pour the milkshake into a glass and garnish with a little more fig. Serve immediately.

SERVES: 8 | PREP TIME: 15 MINS | COOKING TIME: 50 MINS

Banana Loaf Cake

4 very ripe bananas

100 g / 3 ½ oz / ½ cup soft light
   brown sugar

2 large eggs

125 ml / 4 ½ fl. oz / ½ cup sunflower oil

225 g / 8 oz / 1 ½ cups plain
   (all purpose) flour

3 tsp baking powder

1. Preheat the oven to 160°C (140°C fan)
   / 325F / gas 3 and line a loaf tin with
   greaseproof paper.
2. Mash three of the bananas roughly
   with a fork then whisk in the sugar,
   eggs and oil.
3. Sieve the flour and baking powder
   into the bowl and add stir just
   enough to evenly mix all of the
   ingredients together.
4. Scrape the mixture into the loaf tin.
5. Cut the final banana in half
   lengthways and press it into the top.
   Bake for 50 minutes or until a skewer
   inserted comes out clean.
6. Transfer the cake to a wire rack and
   leave to cool completely.
7. This cake will keep for several days in
   an air-tight container.

MAKES: **9** | PREP TIME: **20 MINS** | COOKING TIME: **35 MINS**

Pecan and Marshmallow Brownies

100 g / 3 ½ oz / ⅔ cup dark chocolate (minimum 70% cocoa solids), chopped

85 g / 3 oz / ¾ cup unsweetened cocoa powder, sifted

225 g / 8 oz / 1 cup butter

450 g / 1 lb / 2 ½ cups light brown sugar

4 large eggs

100 g / 3 ½ oz / 1 cup self-raising flour

75 g / 2 ½ oz / ½ cup pecan nuts, roughly chopped

75 g / 2 ½ oz / ½ cup milk chocolate chips

75 g / 2 ½ oz / 1 ¼ cups mini marshmallows

1. Preheat the oven to 160°C (140°C fan) / 325F / gas 3 and oil and line a 20 cm (8 in) square cake tin with greaseproof paper.

2. Melt the chocolate, cocoa and butter together in a saucepan, then leave to cool a little.

3. Whisk the sugar and eggs together with an electric whisk for 3 minutes or until very light and creamy. Pour in the chocolate mixture and sieve over the flour, then add the chocolate chips and half of the pecans. Fold together until evenly mixed, being careful not to knock out too much air.

4. Scrape into the prepared tin and sprinkle over the marshmallows and reserved nuts.

5. Bake for 35 minutes or until the outside is set, but the centre is still quite soft, as it will continue to cook in the residual heat.

6. Leave the brownie to cool completely before cutting into nine squares.

7. These brownies will keep for several days in an air-tight container.

MAKES: 12 | PREP TIME: 20 MINS | COOKING TIME: 15 MINS

Blueberry Jam Cupcakes

110 g / 4 oz / ⅔ cup self-raising flour, sifted
110 g / 4 oz / ½ cup caster (superfine) sugar
110 g / 4 oz / ½ cup butter, softened
2 large eggs
1 tsp vanilla extract
100 ml / 3 ½ fl. oz / ½ cup blueberry jam (jelly)
fresh blueberries, to serve

1. Preheat the oven to 190°C (170°C fan) / 375F / gas 5 and line a 12-hole cupcake tin with paper cases.
2. Combine the flour, sugar, butter, eggs and vanilla extract in a bowl and whisk together for 2 minutes or until smooth.
3. Divide the mixture between the cases and add a spoonful of jam to each one.
4. Bake for 15 minutes or until a skewer inserted comes out clean.
5. Transfer the cakes to a wire rack and leave to cool completely, before serving with fresh blueberries.
6. These cupcakes will keep for several days in an air-tight container.

MAKES: **800 ML** | PREP TIME: **15 MINS** | FREEZING TIME: **3 HOURS**

Banana Smoothie Ice Cream

4 ripe bananas, sliced, plus extra
  to garnish
500 ml / 17 ½ fl. oz / 2 cups
  natural yogurt
250 ml / 9 fl. oz / 1 cup milk
2 tbsp runny honey
2 tbsp pecan nuts, chopped
2 tbsp milk chocolate, grated
mint leaves, to garnish

1. Put the bananas in a liquidizer with
   the yogurt, milk and honey and then
   blend until very smooth.
2. Pour the smoothie into a plastic box
   with a lid and freeze for 2 hours.
3. Scrape the semi-frozen mixture into a
   food processor and blend until
   smooth, then return it to the plastic
   box and freeze for 1 hour.
4. Whizz the mixture in the food
   processor again, then freeze until
   completely firm.
5. Scoop the ice cream into bowls and
   garnish with sliced banana, chopped
   pecans, grated chocolate and
   mint sprigs.

Summer Berry Fool

300 g / 10 ½ oz / 2 cups mixed berries,
plus a few extra to garnish

100 g / 3 ½ oz / ½ cup caster
(superfine) sugar

300 ml / 10 ½ fl. oz / 1 ¼ cups double
(heavy) cream

1 tsp vanilla extract

300 ml / 10 ½ fl. oz / 1 ¼ cups
Greek yogurt

mint leaves, to garnish

1. Put the berries in a saucepan with the sugar. Cover and simmer for 8 minutes,
   stirring half way through.
2. Pass the berries through a sieve to remove the seeds and skins and set aside to cool.
3. Whip the cream with the vanilla extract until it holds its shape, then fold in the
   cooled berry puree and yogurt.
4. Spoon into six dessert glasses and garnish with berries and mint.

Fruit Salad

1 small melon, peeled, deseeded and
cut into bite-sized chunks

3 nectarines, stoned and cut into
bite-sized chunks

1 small bunch grapes, stems removed

225 g / 8 oz / 1 ½ cups fresh or frozen
berries, defrosted if frozen

mint sprigs, to garnish

1. Wash the fruit and dry it using a sheet of kitchen roll.
2. Mix all of the fruits together in a large bowl.
3. Divide between six bowls or wide mugs and garnish with mint.

MAKES: **12** | PREP TIME: **25 MINS** | COOKING TIME: **20 MINS**

Chocolate Muffins

1 large egg
120 ml / 4 fl. oz / ½ cup sunflower oil
120 ml / 4 fl. oz / ½ cup milk
375 g / 12 ½ oz / 2 ½ cups self-raising flour, sifted
1 tsp baking powder
200 g / 7 oz / ¾ cup caster (superfine) sugar
100 g / 3 ½ oz / ⅔ cup dark chocolate, min. 60 per cent cocoa solids, chopped

1. Preheat the oven to 180°C (160°C fan) / 350F / gas 4 and line a 12-hole muffin tin with paper cases.
2. Beat the egg in a jug with the oil and milk until well mixed.
3. Mix the flour, baking powder and sugar in a bowl, then pour in the egg mixture and chopped chocolate and stir just enough to combine.
4. Divide the mixture between the paper cases, then bake in the oven for 20 minutes. Test with a skewer, if it comes out clean, the cakes are done. If not, return to the oven for 5 minutes and test again.
5. Transfer the cakes to a wire rack and leave to cool before serving.
6. These muffins will keep for several days in an air-tight container.

MAKES: 4 | PREP TIME: 30 MINS | COOKING TIME: 1 HOUR | COOLING: 1 HOUR

Salted Caramel Berry Pavlovas

4 large egg whites

110g / 4 oz / 1 cup caster (superfine) sugar

300 g / 10 ½ oz / 2 cups mixed summer berries

300 ml / 10 ½ fl. oz / 1 ¼ cups double (heavy) cream

mint sprigs, to garnish

FOR THE SALTED CARAMEL SAUCE

100 g / 3 ½ oz / ½ cup butter

100 g / 3 ½ oz / ½ cup muscovado sugar

100 g / 3 ½ oz / ⅓ cup golden syrup

100 ml / 3 ½ fl. oz / ½ cup double cream

½ tsp sea salt

1. Preheat the oven to 140°C (120°C fan) / 275F / gas 1 and oil and line two large baking trays with greaseproof paper.
2. Whisk the egg whites until stiff, then gradually whisk in half the sugar until the mixture is very shiny. Fold in the remaining sugar then spread the mixture into six discs on each baking tray.
3. Transfer the trays to the oven and bake for 1 hour, then turn off the heat and leave them to cool completely in the oven.
4. While the meringues are cooling, put all of the sauce ingredients in a small saucepan and stir over a low heat until the sugar dissolves.
5. Bring to the boil then take off the heat and leave to cool.
6. When you're ready to serve, whip the cream until it just holds its shape and sandwich the meringues together in threes, decorating with berries as you go.
7. Drizzle a little sauce over each one and garnish with mint, then serve the rest of the sauce on the side.

Sides and Snacks

SERVES: **6** | PREP TIME: **5 MINS** | COOKING TIME: **20 MINS**

Tomato and Sweetcorn Salsa

2 tbsp olive oil

1 onion, finely chopped

2 cloves of garlic, crushed

400 g / 14 oz / 2 cups canned
   tomatoes, chopped

200 g / 7 oz / 1 cup canned
   sweetcorn, drained

1 tsp caster (superfine) sugar

2 tbsp pickled jalapenos, finely chopped

1 tbsp coriander (cilantro), chopped

tortilla chips, to serve

1. Heat the oil in a saucepan and fry the onion for 5 minutes, stirring occasionally. Add the garlic and stir-fry for 2 more minutes.
2. Add the tomatoes and sweetcorn and simmer for 10 minutes, then stir in the sugar and jalapenos.
3. Season to taste with salt and pepper, then leave to cool and chill in the fridge.
4. Scatter the salsa with coriander before serving with tortilla chips on the side.

MAKES: **12** | PREP TIME: **15 MINS** | COOKING TIME: **25 MINS**

Fennel and Chilli Sausage Rolls

350 g / 12 oz / 2 cups sausagemeat
1 clove of garlic, crushed
1 tsp chilli (chili) flakes
1 ½ tbsp fennel seeds
500 g / 1 lb 2 oz all-butter puff pastry
1 egg, beaten

1. Preheat the oven to 230°C (210°C fan) / 450F / gas 8.
2. Mix the sausagemeat with the garlic, chilli flakes and 1 tsp of the fennel seeds.
3. Roll out the pastry on a lightly floured surface into a large rectangle and cut in half lengthways.
4. Shape the sausagemeat into two long sausages the length of the pastry strips, then fold over the pastry to enclose.
5. Seal the edge with beaten egg and roll so that the join is underneath. Cut each long roll into six pieces and transfer to a baking tray lined with greaseproof paper.
6. Brush the tops with beaten egg and sprinkle with the rest of the fennel seeds, then bake for 25 minutes or until golden brown and cooked through.

Roasted Butternut Squash

3 small butternut squashes, halved
  and deseeded
50 ml / 1 ¾ fl. oz / ¼ cup olive oil

1. Preheat the oven to 200°C (180°C fan) / 400F / gas 6 and line a baking tray with greaseproof paper.
2. Arrange the squash halves cut side up on the baking tray and drizzle with oil. Season generously with salt and pepper.
3. Roast the squash for 45 minutes or until a skewer slides easily into the thickest part.

Scandinavian Potato Salad

6 medium potatoes, peeled and cut
  into chunks
4 large eggs
½ lemon, juiced and zest finely grated
150 ml / 5 ½ fl. oz / ⅔ cup mayonnaise
6 radishes, halved and sliced
1 small bunch dill, chopped

1. Boil the potatoes in salted water for 12 minutes or until tender to the point of a knife. Drain well and leave to cool.
2. Meanwhile, put the eggs in a small saucepan of cold water. When they start to boil, reduce the heat to its lowest setting and simmer gently for 5 minutes. Plunge the eggs into iced water to cool for 5 minutes, then peel, quarter and slice them.
3. Stir the lemon juice and zest into the mayonnaise and season with salt, then toss with the potatoes, eggs, radishes and dill.
4. Serve immediately at room temperature for the best texture, or store in the fridge until later.

SERVES: **4** | PREP TIME: **1 HOUR 35 MINS** | COOKING TIME: **15 MINS**

Homemade Chips

4 large Maris Piper potatoes, peeled and
  cut into skinny chips
sunflower oil for deep-frying
ketchup, to serve

1. Soak the potatoes in cold water for
   1 hour to reduce the starch.
2. Drain the chips and dry completely
   with a clean tea towel, then air-dry
   on a wire rack for 30 minutes.
3. Heat the oil in a deep fat fryer,
   according to the manufacturer's
   instructions, to a temperature of
   130°C (265F). Par-cook the chips for
   10 minutes so that they cook all the
   way through but don't brown.
   Drain the chips on plenty of kitchen
   paper to absorb the excess oil.
4. Increase the fryer temperature to
   190°C (375F).
5. Return the chips to the fryer basket
   and cook for 4 minutes or until crisp
   and golden brown.
6. Drain the chips of excess oil on
   kitchen paper and serve straight away
   with ketchup for dipping.

SERVES: 4 | PREP TIME: 5 MINS | COOKING TIME: 25 MINS

Sweet Potato Wedges with Onion and Feta

3 medium sweet potatoes, peeled and cut into wedges

1 red onion, peeled and cut into wedges

50 ml / 1 ¾ fl. oz / ¼ cup olive oil

1 lemon, zest finely pared

a few sprigs oregano, stems removed

a few sprigs young tender rosemary, stems removed

100 g / 3 ½ oz / ½ cup feta, crumbled

1. Preheat the oven to 220°C (200°C fan) / 425F / gas 7 and line two large baking trays with greaseproof paper.

2. Divide the sweet potato wedges and onion between the two baking trays, drizzle with oil and season with salt and pepper. Toss well to coat.

3. Roast for 25 minutes, turning occasionally, until golden brown and cooked through.

4. Transfer the vegetables to a warm serving dish and toss with the lemon zest, oregano, rosemary and feta. Serve immediately.

Oven-baked Beetroot Crisps

4 medium beetroot, peeled
50 ml / 1 ¾ fl. oz / ¼ cup olive oil
hummus, to serve
salt and pepper

1. Preheat the oven to 140°C (120°C fan) / 275F / gas 1 and line two large baking trays with greaseproof paper.
2. Cut the beetroot into 3 mm slices with a mandolin or a food processor with a slicing attachment. Tip them into a large bowl and drizzle with the oil, then massage it in as evenly as possible.
3. Spread the beetroot slices out on the baking trays and season with salt and pepper. Bake the crisps for 1 hour 30 minutes or until crispy, stirring regularly.
4. Transfer the crisps to two large wire racks and leave to cool completely before serving or storing in an airtight container.

Hummus

400 g / 14 oz / 2 ⅔ cups canned chickpeas (garbanzo beans), drained
90 ml / 3 fl. oz / ⅔ cup olive oil, plus extra to garnish
1 tbsp tahini paste
1 lemon, juiced
1 clove of garlic, crushed
1 pinch smoked paprika

1. Put the chickpeas in a food processor with the oil, tahini, lemon juice and garlic.
2. Blend to a smooth puree, then season to taste with salt and pepper.
3. Spoon into a bowl and garnish a sprinkle of smoked paprika and an extra drizzle of oil.

SERVES: **4** | PREP TIME: **5 MINS** | COOKING TIME: **55 MINS**

Roasted New Potatoes with Dill

800 g / 1 lb 12 oz / 6 ½ cups new potatoes, halved (or cut into thirds, if large)
75 ml / 2 ½ fl. oz / ⅓ cup olive oil
2 cloves of garlic, finely chopped
1 small bunch dill, chopped

1. Preheat the oven to 200°C (180°C fan) / 400F / gas 6.
2. Boil the potatoes in salted water for 10 minutes then drain well and leave to steam dry for 2 minutes. Meanwhile, put the oil in a large roasting tin in the oven to heat.
3. Add the potatoes to the roasting tin and stir to coat in the oil. Season well with salt and pepper.
4. Roast for 20 minutes, then turn them over. Roast for 15 minutes and toss with the garlic, then return to the oven for 10 minutes or until golden brown and crisp.
5. Sprinkle the potatoes with dill just before serving.

SERVES: **6** | PREP TIME: **20 MINS**

Coleslaw

1 red onion, thinly sliced
1 lemon, juiced
2 carrots, peeled
½ small red cabbage, shredded
1 tsp Dijon mustard
100 ml / 3 ½ fl. oz / ½ cup mayonnaise
flat-leaf parsley, to garnish

1. Put the onion in a bowl with the lemon juice and a pinch of salt. Stir well and leave to macerate for 15 minutes to soften the flavour and texture.

2. Shred the carrot with a julienne tool, mandolin or coarse grater and toss with the cabbage and onion.

3. Stir the mustard into the mayonnaise, then mix the dressing with the shredded vegetables.

4. Garnish with parsley and serve straight away or store in the fridge.

MAKES: **12** | PREP TIME: **15 MINS** | COOKING TIME: **15 MINS**

Cheese, Bacon and Spring Onion Scones

1 tbsp olive oil

3 rashers streaky bacon, finely chopped

75 g / 2 ½ oz / ⅓ cup butter, cubed

150 g / 5 ½ oz / 1 cup self-raising flour, plus extra for dusting

100 g / 3 ½ oz / ⅔ cup wholemeal flour

½ tsp mustard powder

¼ tsp cayenne pepper

3 spring onions (scallions), chopped

150 ml / 5 ½ fl. oz / ⅔ cup milk, plus extra for brushing

100 g / 3 ½ oz / 1 cup Red Leicester cheese, grated

1. Preheat the oven to 220°C (200°C fan) / 425F / gas 7 and line two baking trays with greaseproof paper.
2. Heat the oil in a frying pan and fry the bacon for 2 minutes or until golden brown. Leave to cool.
3. Rub the butter into the two flours, then stir in the mustard powder, cayenne pepper, spring onions and bacon. Add the milk and ¾ of the cheese and mix together into a soft dough, adding a little more milk if necessary.
4. Divide the dough into 12 equal pieces and shape into rough rounds, then spread them out on the baking trays.
5. Brush the scones with milk, sprinkle with the rest of the cheese and bake for 15 minutes or until golden brown and cooked through.
6. Transfer the scones to a wire rack to cool a little before serving warm.

SERVES: **8** | PREP TIME: **25 MINS** | COOKING TIME: **20 MINS**

Dried Fruit Scones

225 g / 8 oz / 1 ½ cups self-raising flour
55 g / 2 oz / ¼ cup butter
75 g / 2 ½ oz / ½ cup dried mixed fruit
150 ml / 5 fl. oz / ⅔ cup whole milk, plus extra for brushing
2 tbsp demerara sugar
butter and jam (jelly) to serve

1. Preheat the oven to 220°C (200°C fan) / 425F / gas 7 and oil a large baking sheet.
2. Sieve the flour into a bowl and rub in the butter until the mixture resembles fine breadcrumbs. Add the mixed fruit and stir in enough milk to bring the mixture together into a soft dough.
3. Shape the dough into a round loaf approximately 2.5 cm (1 in) thick.
4. Brush the top with milk and sprinkle with sugar. Cut into eight wedges and transfer to the prepared baking sheet.
5. Bake in the oven for 20 minutes or until golden brown on top and cooked through. Transfer the scones to a wire rack to cool a little, then serve warm with butter and jam.

Garlic Bread

1 baguette
100 g / 3 ½ oz / ½ cup butter, softened
2 cloves of garlic, crushed
2 tbsp parsley, very finely chopped

1. Preheat the oven to 200°C (180°C fan) / 400F / gas 6.
2. Slice the baguette on the diagonal without cutting all the way through to the bottom.
3. Mix the butter with the garlic and parsley and season with salt and pepper. Spread the mixture over the cut surfaces of the bread. Wrap the baguette in foil.
4. Bake for 15 minutes, then open up the foil and bake for 5 more minutes.

White Cob Loaves

800 g / 1 lb 12 oz / 5 ⅓ cups strong white
   bread flour, plus extra for dusting
2 tsp easy blend dried yeast
1 tbsp caster (superfine) sugar
2 tsp fine sea salt
2 tbsp butter, melted

1. Mix together the flour, yeast, sugar and salt. Stir the butter into 560 ml of warm water then stir it into the dry ingredients.
2. Knead the mixture on a lightly oiled surface for 10 minutes or until smooth and elastic. Leave the dough to rest in an oiled bowl, covered with oiled clingfilm, for 1-2 hours or until doubled in size.
3. Knead for 2 minutes then divide in half. Shape into round loaves and transfer to two oiled baking trays. Cover with oiled clingfilm and leave to prove for 1 hour or until doubled in size.
4. Meanwhile, preheat the oven to 220°C (200°C fan) / 425F / gas 7.
5. Make decorative slashes in the top of the loaves with a sharp knife or scalpel and sprinkle with flour.
6. Bake for 40 minutes or until the loaves sound hollow when you tap them underneath.
7. Transfer to a wire rack and leave to cool completely before cutting.

MAKES: **24** | PREP TIME: **15 MINS** | COOKING TIME: **15 MINS**

Spicy Crunch Biscuits

75 g / 2 ½ oz / ⅓ cup butter, softened
100 g / 3 ½ oz / ⅓ cup golden syrup
225 g / 8 oz / 1 ½ cups self-raising flour
100 g / 3 ½ oz / ½ cup caster
   (superfine) sugar
2 tsp ground ginger
1 tsp ground cinnamon
1 large egg, beaten
2 tbsp demerara sugar

1. Preheat the oven to 180°C (160°C fan) / 350F / gas 4 and line two baking sheets with greaseproof paper.
2. Melt the butter and golden syrup together in a saucepan.
3. Mix the flour, caster sugar and spices together then stir in the melted butter mixture and the beaten egg.
4. Use a teaspoon to portion the mixture onto the baking trays, leaving plenty of room for the biscuits to spread.
5. Sprinkling with demerara sugar and bake for 15 minutes or until golden brown.
6. Transfer the biscuits to a wire rack and leave to cool and harden.

MAKES: 24 | PREP TIME: 20 MINS | COOKING TIME: 12 MINS

Red Velvet Crinkle Cookies

250 g / 9 oz / 1 ¼ cups caster (superfine) sugar

100 g / 3 ½ oz / ½ cup butter, softened

1 tsp vanilla extract

2 tsp red food colouring

2 eggs

250 g / 9 oz / 1 ⅔ cups plain (all-purpose) flour

1 ½ tsp baking powder

30 g unsweetened cocoa powder

100 g / 3 ½ oz / ⅔ cup white chocolate chips

100 g / 3 ½ oz / 1 cup icing (confectioner's) sugar

1. Preheat the oven to 180°C (160°C fan) / 350F / gas 4 and line two baking sheets with greaseproof paper.

2. Cream together the sugar, butter, vanilla extract and food colouring until pale and well whipped then beat in the eggs one at a time.

3. Sieve over the flour, baking powder and cocoa and add the chocolate chips, then stir together until evenly mixed.

4. Shape the mixture into 2.5 cm (1 in) balls and roll in icing sugar to coat. Spread out on the prepared trays, leaving plenty of room to spread.

5. Bake the cookies in batches for 12 minutes or until the edges are starting to brown, but the centres are still chewy. Transfer to a wire rack and leave to cool before serving.

MAKES: **24** | PREP TIME: **20 MINS** | COOKING TIME: **15 MINS**

Rainbow Cookies

225 g / 8 oz / 1 ⅓ cups light brown sugar
100 g / 3 ½ oz / ½ cup caster sugar
175 g / 6 oz / ¾ cup butter, melted
2 tsp vanilla extract
1 egg, plus 1 egg yolk
250 g / 9 oz / 1 ⅔ cups self-raising flour
100 g / 3 ½ oz / ⅔ cup Smarties

1. Preheat the oven to 160°C (140°C fan) / 325F / gas 3 and line two baking sheets with greaseproof paper.
2. Cream together the two sugars, butter and vanilla extract until pale and well whipped then beat in the egg and yolk, followed by the flour and Smarties.
3. Use an ice cream scoop to portion the mixture onto the prepared trays, leaving plenty of room to spread.
4. Bake the cookies in batches for 15 minutes or until the edges are starting to brown, but the centres are still chewy. Transfer to a wire rack and leave to cool.

Oaty Wholemeal Banana Muffins

3 very ripe bananas
110 g / 4 oz / ⅔ cup soft light brown sugar
2 large eggs
120 ml / 4 fl. oz / ½ cup sunflower oil
200 g / 7 oz / 1 ⅓ cups wholemeal flour
2 tsp baking powder
30 g rolled porridge oats, plus extra
    for sprinkling

1. Preheat the oven to 200°C (180°C fan) / 400F / gas 6 and grease a 12-hole silicone cupcake mould.
2. Mash the bananas with a fork then whisk in the sugar, eggs and oil.
3. Sieve the flour and baking powder into the bowl and add the oats, then stir just enough to evenly mix all the ingredients together.
4. Spoon the mixture into the mould and sprinkle with oats.
5. Bake for 18 minutes or until a skewer inserted comes out clean.
6. Transfer the muffins to a wire rack and leave to cool a little before serving.

Gingerbread Biscuits

100 g / 3 ½ oz / ½ cup soft brown sugar
100 g / 3 ½ oz / ½ cup butter, softened
1 large egg, beaten
300 g / 10 ½ oz / 2 cups plain
    (all-purpose) flour
2 tsp ground ginger

1. Cream together the sugar and butter until pale and well whipped then beat in the egg, followed by the flour and ginger. Bring the mixture together into a ball with your hands then wrap in clingfilm and refrigerate for 45 minutes.
2. Preheat the oven to 190°C (170°C fan) / 375F / gas 5 and line two baking sheets with greaseproof paper.
3. Roll out portions of the dough on a lightly floured surface to 3 mm thick. Use a flower-shaped cutter to cut out the biscuits, rerolling the trimmings as necessary.
4. Transfer the biscuits to the prepared trays in batches and bake for 10 minutes or until cooked through and golden brown. Transfer the biscuits to a wire rack and leave to cool completely.
5. These will keep for several days in an air-tight container.

SERVES: 6 | PREP TIME: 20 MINS | COOKING TIME: 30 MINS

Churros and Hot Chocolate

100 g / 3 ½ oz / ½ cup butter
150 g / 5 ½ oz / 1 cup plain (all-purpose) flour
3 medium eggs, beaten
75 g / 2 ½ oz / ⅓ cup caster (superfine) sugar
sunflower oil, for deep-frying

FOR THE HOT CHOCOLATE
500 ml / 17 ½ fl. oz / 2 cups whole milk
100 g / 3 ½ oz / ⅔ cup dark chocolate (min. 60 per cent cocoa solids), grated
1 tbsp cornflour (cornstarch)
50 g / 1 ¾ oz / ¼ cup caster (superfine) sugar

1. Heat the butter in a saucepan with 250 ml of water and ¼ a teaspoon of salt. When it boils rapidly, beat in the flour, then stir over a low heat until it forms a ball that leaves the pan clean.
2. Take the saucepan off the heat and leave to cool a little, then beat in the eggs.
3. Heat the oil in a deep fat fryer, according to the manufacturer's instructions, to a temperature of 180°C (350F).
4. Transfer the Churros mixture to a piping bag fitted with a large star nozzle. Pipe four 10 cm (4 in) strips of dough into the hot oil and cook for 4 minutes, turning halfway through.
5. Remove the churros from the fryer and drain on kitchen paper, then roll in caster sugar to coat. Continue to fry the churros in batches of four until all the mixture has been used.
6. Meanwhile, heat 400 ml of milk until it starts to simmer, then whisk in the grated chocolate. Stir the cornflour into the remaining 100 ml of cold milk, then stir it into the pan with the sugar. Continue to stir until the chocolate thickens, then divide between six cups and serve with the Churros.

SERVES: 10 | PREP TIME: **20 MINS** | COOKING TIME: **25 MINS**

Gluten-free Granola Bars

100 g / 3 ½ oz / ½ cup butter

100 g / 3 ½ oz / ⅓ cup runny honey

75 g / 2 ½ oz / ⅓ cup light muscovado sugar

175 g / 6 oz / 1 ¾ cups rolled buckwheat flakes

50 g / 1 ¾ oz / ½ cup sunflower seeds

50 g / 1 ¾ oz / ½ cup pumpkin seeds

50 g / 1 ¾ oz / ¼ cup sesame seeds

100 g / 3 ½ oz / ¾ cup walnuts, chopped

100 g / 3 ½ oz / ½ cup raisins

50 g / 1 ¾ oz / ½ cup ground almonds

1. Preheat the oven to 180°C (160°C fan) / 350F / gas 4 and grease and line a 20 x 30 cm (8 in x 11 in) tray bake tin with greaseproof paper.
2. Put the butter, honey and sugar in a saucepan and melt them together over a low heat until the sugar dissolves. Increase the heat and bubble for 1 minute.
3. Take the pan off the heat and stir in the rest of the ingredients with a pinch of salt.
4. Tip the mixture into the prepared tin and press it into an even layer.
5. Bake in the oven for 25 minutes, or until golden brown.
6. Cut the tray bake into bars while it is still warm, but leave to cool completely in the tin before serving.

Strawberry Smoothie

100 g / 3 ½ oz / ⅔ cup strawberries, sliced
2 tbsp Greek yogurt
75 ml / 2 ½ fl. oz / ⅓ cup apple juice
1 tsp runny honey
4 ice cubes

1. Reserve a few sliced strawberries for a garnish and put the rest in a liquidizer with the rest of the ingredients.
2. Blend for 1 minute or until very smooth.
3. Pour into a glass and garnish with the reserved sliced strawberries.

Green Super Smoothie

2 bananas, chopped
2 kiwi fruit, peeled and chopped
35 g baby leaf spinach
250 ml / 9 fl. oz / 1 cup apple juice

1. Spread the banana and kiwi fruit out on a greaseproof paper lined baking tray and freeze for at least 2 hours. It can then be transferred to a freezer bag and stored for future use or used straight away.
2. Put the spinach in a liquidizer with the apple juice. Blend until smooth.
3. Add the frozen banana and kiwi and blend again until smooth, then pour into a glass and serve immediately.

Index